The 20-Minute
CHORDS
& HaRMony

WORKOUT

By Stuart Isacoff

About The Author

Pianist and composer Stuart Isacoff is the founding editor of Keyboard Classics Magazine and consulting editor of Sheet Music Magazine and The Piano Stylist. He is a recipient of the ASCAP Deems Taylor Award for excellence in writing about music, and has authored over twenty music books. His work is published by G. Schirmer, Boosey & Hawkes, Associated Music Publishers, Music Sales Corp., Carl Fischer, and Ekay Music.

Table Of Contents

INTRO

"You don't have to be a magician to master the art of harmony."

*H*armony — *the combination of three or more tones played simultaneously* — is a subject as wide and as fascinating as the rainbow of colors these shifting sounds produce in the best of pop, jazz and classical music. Listen to any great melody by Brahms, Gershwin, or Billy Joel without the help of its harmonic "foundation." Then add the accompanying chords . . . MAGIC!

But you don't have to be a magician to master the art of harmony. There are only 12 different tones, after all, and if you play a keyboard you're already very acquainted with them all. The best way to learn about harmony is through example and a bit of practice . . . about 20 minutes a day. As long as the subject matter is approached in a step-by-step manner, anyone can become an "expert." And here is your first lesson . . .

Day 1

▶ **A QUICK LOOK AT INTERVALS   8 MINUTES**

Before taking a look at combinations involving three, four, five, six and even more tones played at once, let's review the kinds of two-tone arrangements (*intervals*) that are possible. The first and easiest is the unison. Play C:

Now play C:

> *"These are the basic building blocks of chords."*

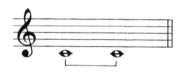

That was a unison.
Next we have the octave. Play C:

Now play a C major scale ascending. Count C as scale tone number one, and continue until you come to number eight:

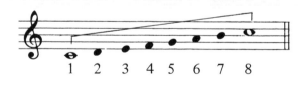

That was an octave. Counting scale tones to number fifteen will produce an interval two octaves apart:

6

Counting to tone number four produces the interval of a fourth:

Counting up from tone number one to tone number six produces the interval of a sixth:

Counting scale tones will show us the full variety of "flavorings" our chords can contain. For example, most chords will include thirds:

and fifths:

and perhaps sevenths:

even ninths:

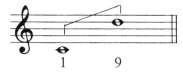

These are the basic building blocks of chords. We'll see later that there are in fact different *kinds* of fifths, thirds, ninths and so on. But in the beginning we're going to start with the most basic elements of harmony; in order to prepare for work with the primary chords used in western harmony, it is essential to practice the intervals used to build them.

▶ **SOME INTERVAL EXERCISES**   **12 MINUTES**

In each of the following major scales, find the intervals asked for. Always begin on the starred (*) note. (For the correct answers, turn to the end of the chapter.)

1) Find the 3rd:

2) Find the octave:

3) Find the sixth:

4) Find the fourth:

5) Find the seventh:

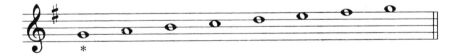

6) Find the fifth:

9

7) Find the third:

8) Find the second:

9) Find the ninth:

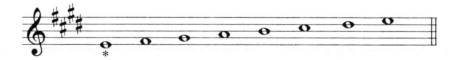

10) Find the fifth:

11) Find the fourth:

12) Find the sixth:

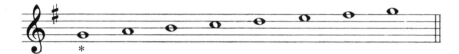

13) Find the third:

14) Find the third:

15) Find the fifth:

Day 2

The first chord on our list is the major chord — a triad (three note chord) built by starting on the first note of any major scale, and including the interval of a third above that note, and the interval of a fifth above it (these are, of course, scale tones 1, 3 and 5):

In pop music, a kind of shorthand is often used to indicate harmonies. The shorthand symbol for a C major chord is C.

Here are several major scales. Practice building a major triad on the first note of each of these.

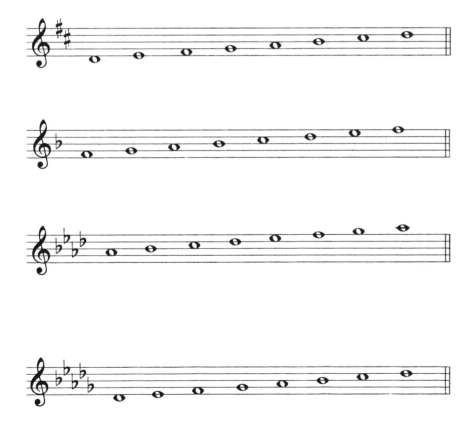

"Chords are present as 'hidden melodies' in many well-known pieces."

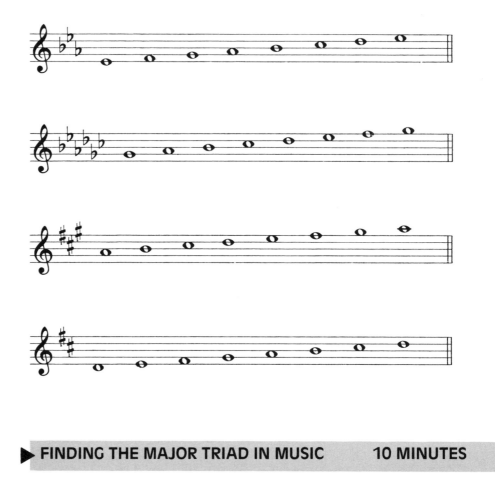

► **FINDING THE MAJOR TRIAD IN MUSIC**   **10 MINUTES**

Play the C major triad we formed earlier once again. It's probably a sound you've heard thousands of times. But chords are also present as "hidden melodies" in many, many well known pieces.

The sound of a major triad will be familiar, for example, to anyone who has heard traditional trumpet fanfares, such as this horn call used at the racetrack:

or the soldier's dreaded morning *Reveille:*

14

or *Taps:*

These are all *arpeggiated,* or broken versions of the major triad. So is the opening of the "Star Spangled Banner":

and of this Sonata for violin and piano by Ludwig van Beethoven:

The tones of the major triad are, of course, also played together as a chord. Here is an example from Wolfgang Amadeus Mozart's opera *The Magic Flute:*

But it is as a melody that these tones will be most helpful to work with at this point, because those triadic melodies show us that the scale steps that make up a major chord do not always appear in the order 1, 3, 5 (notice what the lowest note is for the racetrack fanfare). So for the remainder of this 10-minute segment, practice playing all of the following major chords as arpeggios (follow the example given for the C chord):

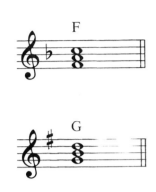

Day 3

▶ MORE ARPEGGIOS   20 MINUTES

Continuing our practice of isolating major chord tones, here are more major harmonies to arpeggiate. By spending some time becoming thoroughly familiar with these chords, you will make mastering the art of keyboard harmony an easier task. Follow the first example.

"Practice in isolating major chord tones makes mastering the art of keyboard harmony easier."

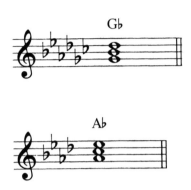

Day 4

▶ INVERSIONS   12 MINUTES

When the notes of a chord appear on the keyboard in an order other than 1, 3, 5, the chord is said to be in an "inversion." We'll see in a moment what the major chords look like when they are inverted. But in order to prepare for our inversion study, and to make the notes of each major chord even more familiar, let's turn again to the melody of *Reveille*.

"There are actually three different shapes that a major chord may appear in."

As we saw earlier, these melody notes make up a C major triad. We can find all the other major chords as well, simply by "transposing" this melody — that is, by beginning it on other pitches. In order to play the tune on an F major chord, we can transpose it to the key of F. Since the melody began on the fifth of the C chord, we must now begin it on the fifth degree of the F scale.

Write out and play this tune in the keys of Bb, D, A and G. Then play the major triad in each case as a block chord, rather than as an arpeggio (as in the examples in C and F).

20

▶ AT THE ROOT   8 MINUTES

There are actually three different shapes that a major chord may appear in. The first, with which we began, is constructed of the chord "root" (tone 1 of the scale for which it is named), the third (tone 3) and the fifth (tone 5):

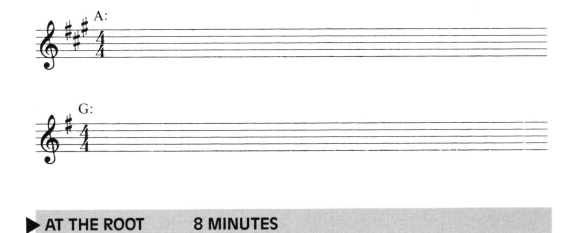

It is said to be in *root position.*
Here are root position major triads in several keys.

21

Complete the chord catalogue below by filling in the missing root position harmonies:

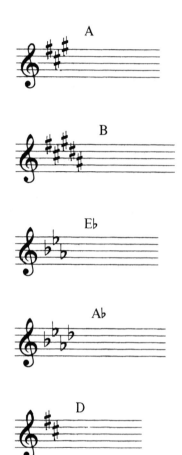

Day 5

The second shape or chord position occurs when the *third* of the chord appears on the *bottom*. It is said to be in *first inversion:*

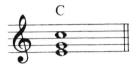

Create a first inversion chord chart by filling in the blanks below. Don't forget to add accidentals where needed.

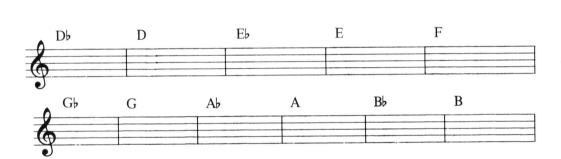

> *"The second shape or chord position is known as* first inversion.*"*

▶ GETTING ON FIRST   10 MINUTES

Now play all of the major triads in first inversion. Follow the example of the C chord below.

Day 6

▶ BOTTOMS UP   10 MINUTES

The last shape that triads may be found in has the *fifth* on the bottom. It is referred to as being in *second inversion.* Many organists and pianists find this inversion particularly helpful in voicing chords so that all the notes fall within or lie close to the keyboard range between middle C and the C below it. Playing chords within that keyboard range is almost a rule of thumb for pianists working with a bass player.

> *"Many organists and pianists find this inversion particularly helpful in voicing chords."*

Place the following chords in second inversion by building them with their fifths (tone 5 of the scale to which they belong) on the bottom:

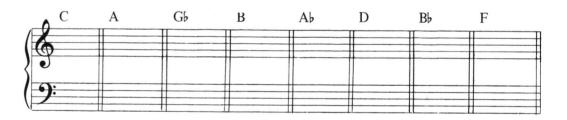

▶ POSITION IS WHAT COUNTS!   10 MINUTES

Now let's mix it up a bit. Here's a game that will allow you to test your skills in spotting chord inversions. Just look at each example, decide what major chord you are looking at, and determine whether it is in root position, or if not, what inversion it is in. See how quickly you can make your decisions!

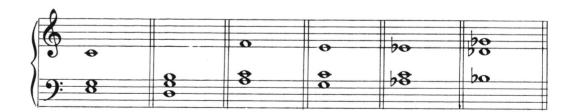

24

25

Day 7

This famous little melody by Mozart demonstrates that shifting bass notes may change the inversion of a particular harmony rapidly within a musical piece; all three inversions appear here within a single measure.

> *"Composers and arrangers will often change the placement of a chord to produce a particular effect."*

It's important to remember that chord inversions are defined by which chord tone is on the *bottom*. This is worth emphasizing because composers and arrangers will often change the placement of chord tones to produce a particular effect *without* altering the chord's inversion. For example, in order to avoid a muddy sound, an arranger might "voice" the following C Major chord:

like this:

The order of the chord tones has been changed, but the chord is still in *root* position, because the root (tone 1 of the scale) has remained on the bottom.

26

Similarly, here are two versions of a C Major chord in first inversion. In both cases, the bottom note is E (the third of the chord).

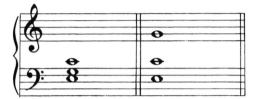

In order to be able to recognize the names of chords that are voiced in different ways, use the following two drills. They will help you to see through the "disguises" of chords that are changed through "voicing" techniques.

▶ PLAY AND SAY   8 MINUTES

Play the following major chords in both voicings up and down the keyboard. Say the name of the chord as you play.

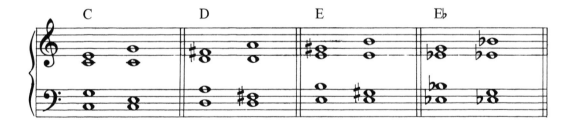

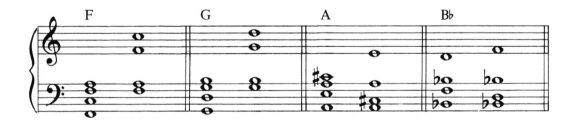

►CHORDS IN DISGUISE   8 MINUTES

Name the following major chords. Indicate both the chord and whether it is in root position, first inversion, or second inversion. For the correct answers, see below.

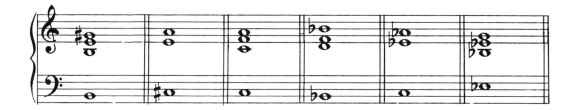

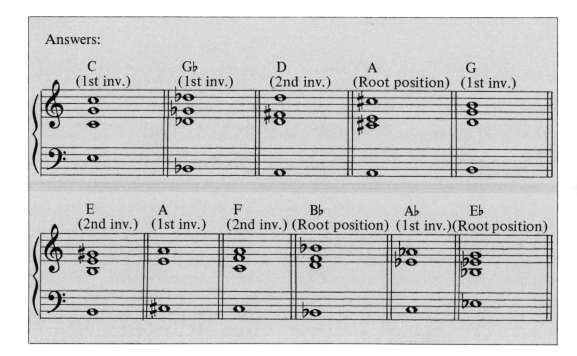

Day 8

▶ CHORD PROGRESSIONS   10 MINUTES

Music does not, of course, consist of just static chords, but of a series of harmonies. In order to describe the way in which chords follow each other in a piece of music (the chord *progression)*, musicians have assigned numbers to the chords built on various members of the scale that is used as the key center of a piece. If a piece is in the key of C, for example, the chords are numbered according to which tones of the C major scale they are built on. When chords are numbered in this way, they are labeled with Roman Numerals.

The chord built on step one of the major scale is called the *tonic* or I chord. It is one of three *primary* chords in any key. The I chord in the key of C is the C major chord; in the key of F it is the F major chord; in the key of G it is the G major chord.

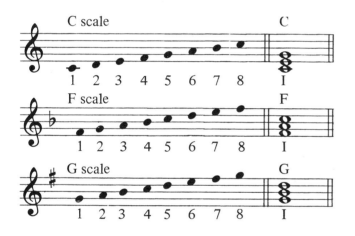

"In order to describe the way in which chords follow each other, musicians have assigned them special numbers."

The chord built on step four of the major scale is called the *subdominant* or IV chord. The IV chord in the key of C is the F major chord; in the key of F it is the Bb major chord; in the key of G it is the C major chord.

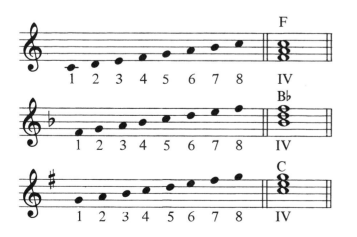

The chord built on step five of the major scale is called the *dominant* or V chord. The V chord in the key of C is the G major chord; in the key of F it is the C major chord; in the key of G it is the D major chord.

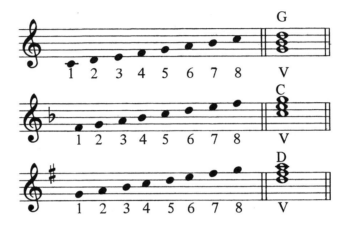

The I, IV and V chords in any major key will always be major chords.

To practice calling these chords by their correct labels, name the IV chords in the following keys:

Name the V chords in the following keys:

Many folk songs use only the I, IV and V chords. Even complex music almost always makes use of the two popular *cadences,* or phrase endings, of V-I (called an "authentic" or "perfect" cadence) and IV-I (referred to as a "plagal" or "gospel" cadence):

For the following keys, write out the I, IV and V chords:

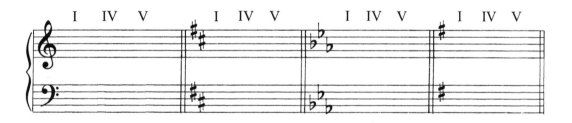

Identify the chords in the following I-IV-V chord progressions.

31

Day 9

It's time to combine some of the concepts already introduced. When chord progressions unfold in a piece of music, it is often necessary for the chords to appear in inversion. The reason is clear in the following examples, where the individual musical lines are made smooth through the use of inversion. Here is a familiar song written first in root position only — notice how choppy the sound is.

"Inversions smooth out the individual musical lines in a song's harmonies."

More satisfying is this version in which the chord roots are not always on the bottom.

32

Now turn to the exercises below for practice in seeing and writing major chord progressions in both root positions and inversions. Chord names are indicated above the staff, and the bass note for each chord is given. Fill in the missing chord members.

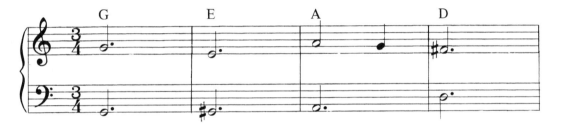

Worksheet

Day 10

Now that you have studied the three primary chords, I, IV and V, in root positions and inversions, you are ready for some "hands on" keyboard harmony experience! Here are melodies and chord symbols given without any indication of which inversion would work best. Try your hand at "instant arranging" by choosing the inversion or root position that will best fill out each tune in a smooth way. (Refer to the suggested solutions *after* you have already worked these out on your own.)

Down In The Valley

"Choose the inversion or root position that will best fill out each tune in a smooth way."

36

The Streets Of Laredo

Sweet Adeline

Suggested Answers:

Down In The Valley

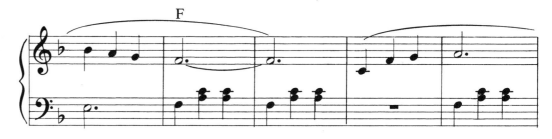

The Streets Of Laredo

Sweet Adeline

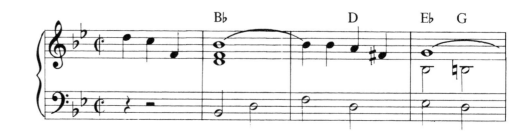

The Clarinet Polka

Day 11

▶ ADDING NEW COLORS!   10 MINUTES

There are many more harmonic colors to explore beyond the major triads. Even among the three-note chords, there are also minor, diminished and augmented harmonies. And once we branch out beyond just three notes, there will be different forms of seventh, ninth, eleventh, thirteenth and even more complex chords. But the basic skills that you have been developing and practicing up to now will make the rest fall into place in a logical, clear manner.

So it's on to minor chords! The minor chord is produced by the simple change of one note in the major chord: the third is moved down ½ step.

"The minor sound is often described as sad, scary or passionate."

The minor sound is often described as sad, or scary or passionate. That's why so many composers have used it in highly dramatic ways. Here, for example, is the famous minor theme from Chopin's "Funeral March."

44

Play a series of major chords:

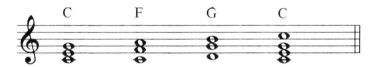

Followed by a series of minor chords:

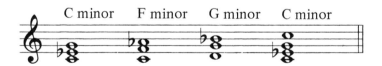

The difference may be described in many ways — any attempt would be completely subjective, of course. But it is clear that there *is* in fact a big difference in the sound. We can call it a difference of color, and most music you play will make use of this basic color contrast between major and minor.

The shorthand symbol for a C minor chord is Cm.

To gain familiarity with this new sound, change the following major chords to minor chords (the C chord is given):

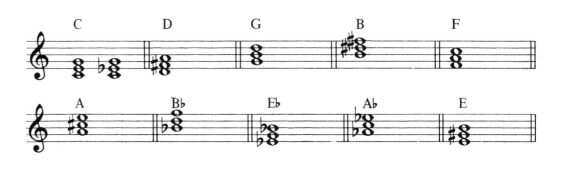

▶ MINOR ARPEGGIOS   10 MINUTES

The minor chords can be broken up in the same way as the major chords, of course, and these arpeggios will help you to picture the tones of the minor harmonies just as you learned to picture the pitches of the major ones. Play and practice these arpeggiated versions of the minor triads:

46

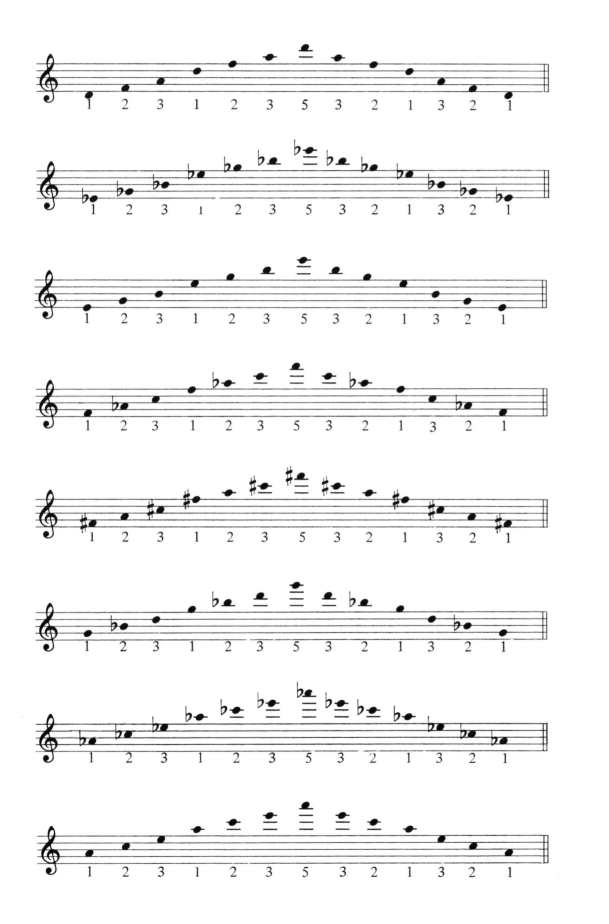

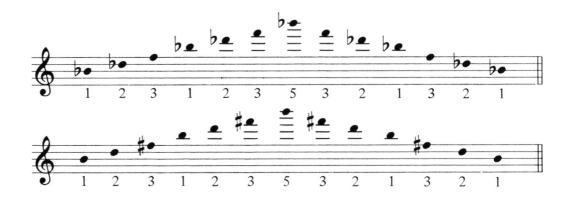

1 2 3 1 2 3 5 3 2 1 3 2 1

1 2 3 1 2 3 5 3 2 1 3 2 1

Day 12

▶ MINOR INVERSIONS   6 MINUTES

The minor chords may appear in inversion just as the major chords do. Day 12 will be devoted to learning the minor inversions. Begin by completing the following chart of minor chords in root position:

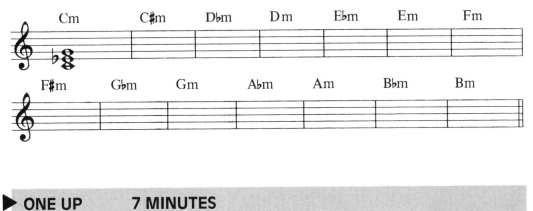

▶ ONE UP   7 MINUTES

Next, finish the following chart of minor chords in first inversion. Remember, these chords will place their *thirds* on the bottom:

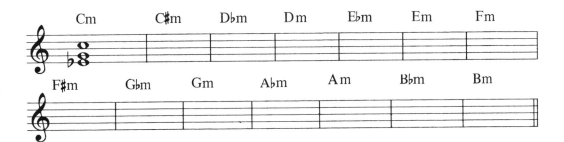

When you've finished your chart, play all the chords several times.

▶ THE LAST STEP   7 MINUTES

Finally, here is a chart for you to complete listing the minor triads in second inversion. These chords will all have their *fifths* on the very bottom:

> *"Minor chords may appear in inversion too."*

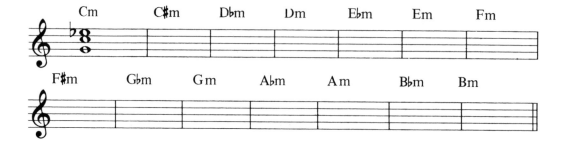

When you've finished, play through the chart until you are certain that you will recognize these chords the next time you see one.

Day 13

▶ DOWN FOR THE COUNT   10 MINUTES

Comparing the intervals, or distances, between the tones in a major chord and those in a minor chord will help us to produce a formula for each of these two chord models. Once we learn this formula we will be able to construct either chord at any time, beginning on any note.

For purposes of building chords up to now, it was sufficient to label our intervals according to their positions in the major scale (octave, fourth and so on). But from this point on we will be working with finer shadings of distances between notes, so it's necessary to use a more detailed method.

That method consists of measuring intervals in terms of two different kinds of "steps" we find between the notes of our scales. The shortest interval we will ever find is the half step: the distance between B and C, for instance, or between C and C#.

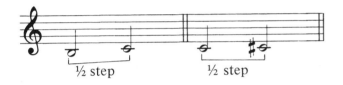
½ step   ½ step

> *"Once we learn their formulas, we will be able to construct either of these chords, beginning on any note."*

Two half steps in a row create a whole step: the interval of C to D, for instance, or that of E to F#.

whole step   whole step

To become comfortable with this method of counting, use the following exercise. Label the intervals by the number of steps they contain.

The distance between tones 1 and 3 in the major scale (that is, the *third*) consists of two whole steps:

To create a minor third, we must decrease the size of that interval by a half step. Therefore, a minor third is 1½ steps in length:

With this information under our belts, it is possible to construct formulas for the major and minor triads. The major chord is made by building a major third (2 steps) and then adding a minor third (1½ steps) on top of it:

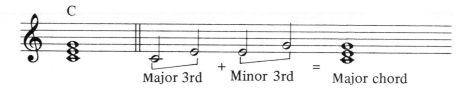

The minor chord is made by stacking those two intervals in the opposite way — first a minor third (1½ steps) and then a major third (2 steps) on top:

Practice building major triads on the following roots, using the formula
MAJOR THIRD + MINOR THIRD:

Day 14

Let's stay in the laboratory for a while longer, and create minor triads on the following roots, using the formula MINOR THIRD + MAJOR THIRD:

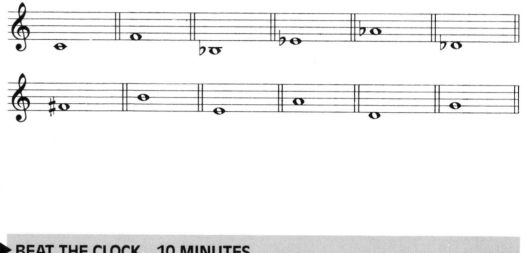

"It's time to test your skills. Check your answers after you've finished."

▶ BEAT THE CLOCK   10 MINUTES

Now that you are thoroughly familiar with major and minor chords, test your skills by playing the following drill *as fast as possible*. As you go through the list below, keep your fingers on the keyboard; as you read the name of each major or minor chord, play it with as little hesitation as possible. You can check your answers on the next page. Good luck!

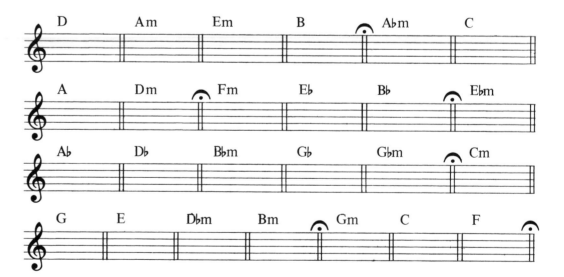

Answers:

(Chords placed in inversion create smoother transitions.)

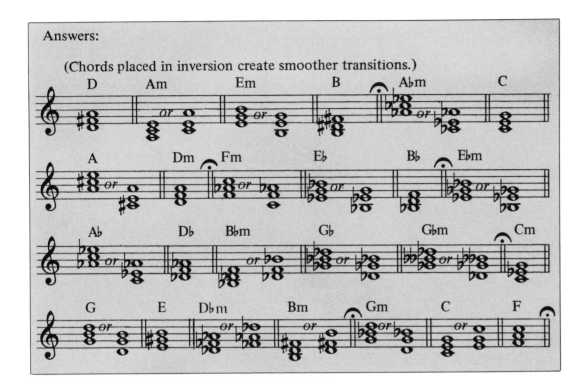

Day 15

The term "to diminish" means to make something less, and in music a diminished interval is one that has been shortened. A diminished fifth, for example, is a perfect fifth (C to G, for instance) that has been shortened by a half step (in this case, C to Gb).

"In music, a diminished interval is one that has been shortened."

Perfect 5th   Diminished 5th

Major intervals that are shortened by a half step become minor intervals (seconds, thirds, sixths, sevenths). *Perfect* intervals (fourths, fifths and octaves) are called diminished when they are shortened by a half step.

Major 3rd   Minor 3rd

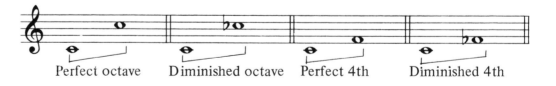

Perfect octave   Diminished octave   Perfect 4th   Diminished 4th

56

Now that we have introduced the diminished fifth, we are ready to learn about diminished *chords!* To produce a diminished chord, simply take any minor triad and move the fifth down one half step. The chord now has a diminished fifth and a minor third.

The symbol in musical shorthand for a C diminished chord is C dim. or C°.

▶ A MINOR MATTER   10 MINUTES

Change the following minor chords to diminished chords. Be sure you "spell" each chord correctly! (Fifths become flatted in order to create the diminished interval.) The first two are spelled for you.

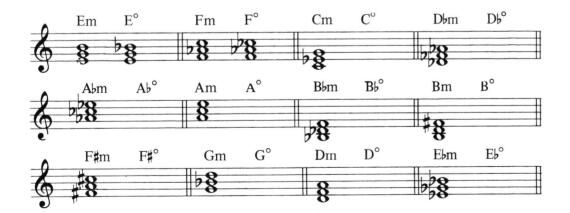

Play the diminished chords you have constructed in the last section in different octaves on the keyboard. Try each chord in several different ranges, hands separately and hands together!

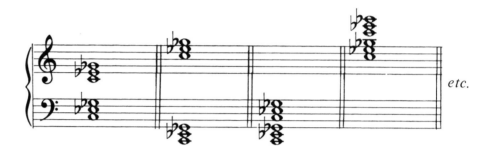

etc.

Day 16

▶ MAJOR, MINOR, DIMINISHED   10 MINUTES

Here's an exercise to help "tune up" to the differences in chord shapes and harmonic colors produced by the three triads we have now covered. Spend as much time as you need to make these chords second nature to you.

Play the following chords as arpeggios. Follow the first examples:

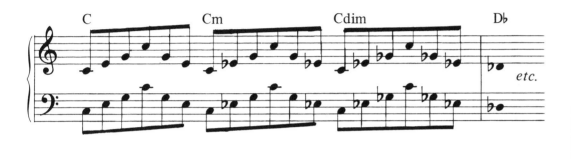

C–C minor–C diminished

Db–Db minor–Db diminished

D–D minor–D diminished

Eb–Eb minor–Eb diminished

"Spend as much time as you need to make these chords second nature to you."

▶ FROM BOTTOM TO TOP   10 MINUTES

Play all twelve diminished chords in first inversion. Follow the example below:

Day 17

▶ MORE ARPEGGIOS   10 MINUTES

Continue the arpeggio exercise begun in DAY 16 with the following chord progressions:

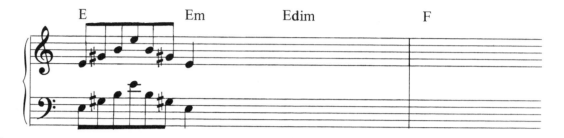

"Here are more chord progressions to help you gain familiarity with these harmonies."

E-E minor-E diminished

F-F minor-F diminished

F#-F# minor-F# diminished

G-G minor-G diminished

▶ FROM TOP TO BOTTOM   10 MINUTES

Play all twelve diminished chords in second inversion. Follow the example below:

Day 18

Complete the arpeggio exercise by playing the following chord progressions. You will now have played the major, minor and diminished chords in all twelve keys.

▶ **A NEW SOUND!**   **10 MINUTES**

You've probably had your fill of major, minor and diminished for a while, so here is a completely new color! It's called an augmented chord.

Just as a diminished interval is formed by a process of *shortening,* an *augmented* interval is formed by means of . . . you guessed it: *lengthening.*

A perfect fifth, say, C to G, becomes an augmented fifth when the G is raised one half step. The augmented fifth is C to G#.

"You've probably had your fill of major, minor and diminished. Here's a completely new color!"

Perfect 5th   Augmented 5th

To form an augmented chord, take any major triad and raise the fifth one half step.

C Major   C Augmented

The musical shorthand used to describe a C augmented chord is C + .

Turn the following major chords into augmented chords. The first one has been done for you.

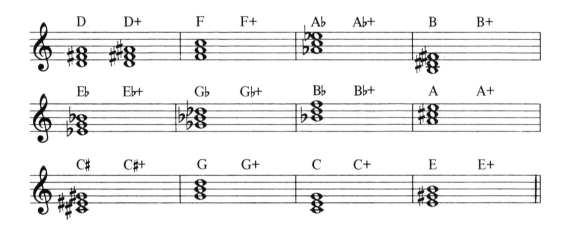

Day 19

▶ **THE SYMMETRY OF SHORT AND LONG**   **10 MINUTES**

To build a major triad, we placed the interval of a minor third over the interval of a major third:

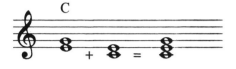

And to build a minor triad we placed the interval of a major third over the interval of a minor third:

> "Two of our chords have a very special quality due to the symmetry of their intervals."

Another way of saying this is that the major triad consists of (counting from the bottom) an interval of two whole steps plus an interval of one and a half steps:

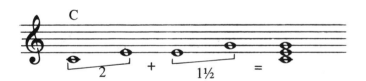

The minor triad, on the other hand, consists of (counting from the bottom) an interval of one and a half steps plus an interval of two whole steps:

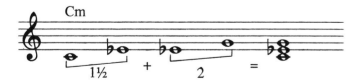

How about the diminished chord? As you can see, it is constructed by placing two minor thirds on top of each other . . . that is, an interval of one and a half steps plus an interval of one and a half steps:

And the augmented chord is constructed by placing two major thirds on top of each other . . . that is, an interval of two whole steps plus an interval of two whole steps:

In the case of the augmented chord, a very special quality emerges from the symmetry of its intervals. The major thirds used to construct this chord divide the octave into three equal parts. As a result, all of the inversions of an augmented chord produce another augmented chord in root position! When a C augmented chord is placed in first inversion, for instance, it produces an augmented chord beginning on E (if we make adjustments for the way the chord is spelled):

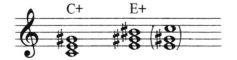

That same C augmented chord in second inversion looks like a G# augmented chord:

So, for all practical purposes, there are really only four different augmented chords (as opposed to twelve different major chords):

C+ = E+ = G#+

C#+ = F+ = A+

D+ = F#+ = A#+

Eb+ = G+ = B+

▶MINOR-MINOR   10 MINUTES

Construct diminished chords beginning on the following pitches, by stacking two minor thirds:

Day 20

▶ **MAJOR-MAJOR**   **10 MINUTES**

Construct augmented chords on the following pitches by stacking two major thirds:

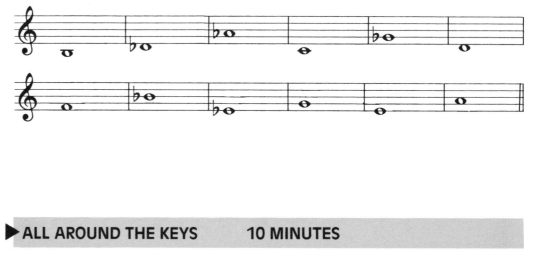

"Here's a more complete chart of the harmonies that can be built from a major scale."

▶ **ALL AROUND THE KEYS**   **10 MINUTES**

We saw earlier how the major chords formed on scale tones I, IV and V relate to each other in *cadences*. Here's another chart of the harmonies that can be built from a major scale, this time including chords II, III, VI and VII.

* *Sometimes minor chords are represented by lower case letters, such as ii for the chord built on tone 2 of the scale.*

Did you note that the chords formed on II, III and VI are all minor chords? And how about the harmony built on tone VII?

Practice forming the correct chord types in the following keys by writing in the harmonies above the Roman numerals:

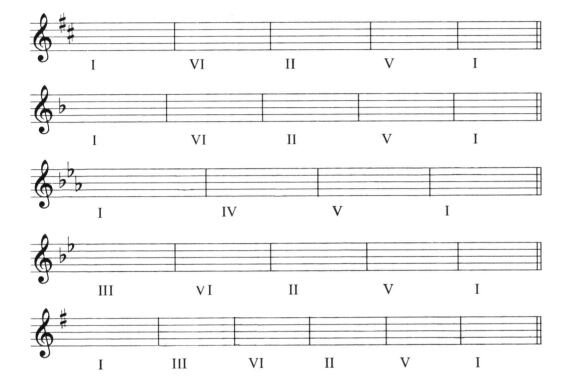

     I   VI   II   V   I

     I   VI   II   V   I

     I   IV   V   I

     III   VI   II   V   I

     I   III   VI   II   V   I

Day 21

Now that the four types of triads are securely understood, it's worthwhile examining a few of the ways in which they are used in real music.

Chords often follow each other in specific patterns called chord progressions. Here are some typical ones. Play through them and study each example until the kind of sounds that result from each chord type clearly registers in your ears. (Note how the augmented and diminished chords are used to "smooth out" the harmonic movement. This is called "voice leading.")

"Ready for some real music? Our four triad types can form typical chord progressions."

I-IV-I

I-V-I

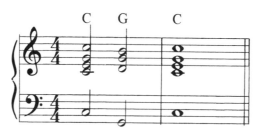

The Blues

68

Folk And Pop Songs

Hot Time In The Old Town Tonight by Joe Hayden and Theo A. Metz

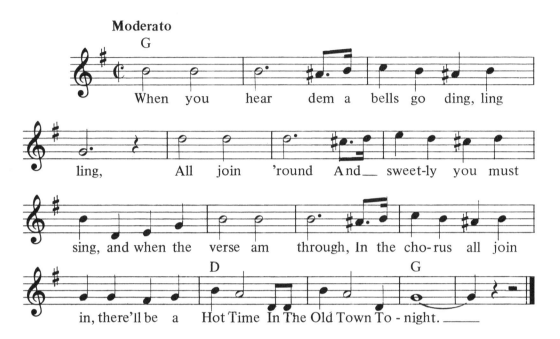

America The Beautiful by Samuel A. Ward

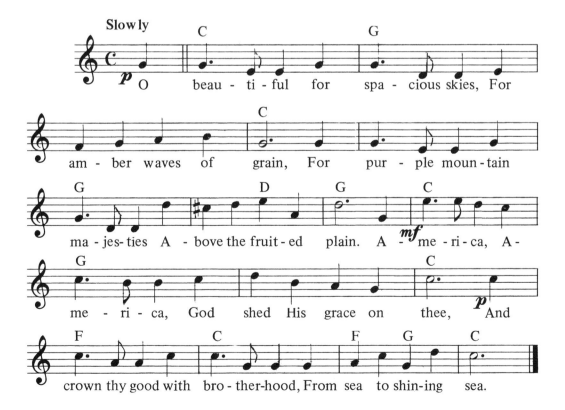

Buffalo Gals

Lively

Buf-fa-lo gals, won't you come out to-night? Come out to-night?

Come out to-night? Buf-fa-lo gals, won't you come out to-night? And

dance by the light of the moon? Dance with a doll with a

hole in her stock-ing, And her toe keeps a-knock-ing, And her

heel keeps a-rock-ing, Gon-na dance with a doll with a

hole in her stock-ing, Gon-na dance by the light of the

moon, Oh! Buf-fa-lo gals, won't you come out to-night?

Come out to-night? Come out to-night? Buf-fa-lo gals, won't you

Come out to-night? And dance by the light of the moon?

70

A Bicycle Built For Two by Harry Dacre

Dai - sy, Dai - sy, give me your an - swer, do! _____ I'm half cra - zy, All for the love of you! _____ It won't be a styl - ish mar - riage, _____ I can't af - ford a car - riage, _____ But you'll look sweet On the seat of a bi - cy - cle built for two. _____

Minor Progressions

Black Is The Color Of My True Love's Hair

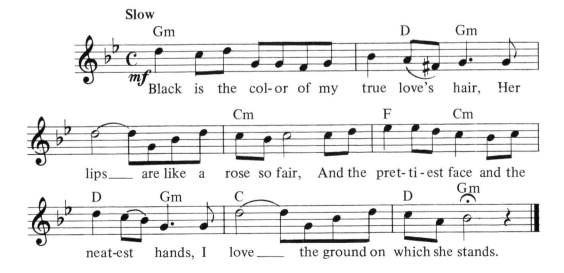

Black is the col - or of my true love's hair, Her lips ____ are like a rose so fair, And the pret - ti - est face and the neat - est hands, I love ____ the ground on which she stands.

71

Greensleeves

Scarborough Fair

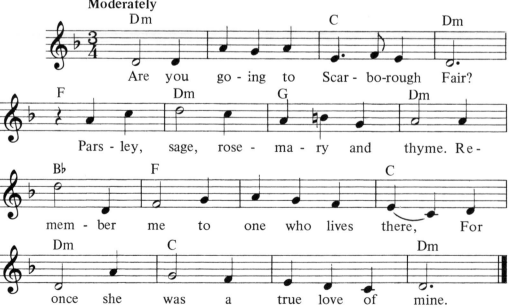

We Three Kings Of Orient Are by John H. Hopkins

Use Of Augmented Harmonies

Aura Lee by W. W. Fosdick and George R. Poulton

Careless Love

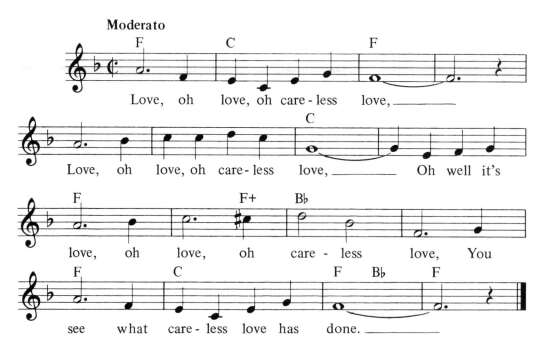

Use Of Diminished Harmonies

Believe Me If All Those Endearing Young Charms

* *Use a G in the bass here, to create the rising bass line F — F♯ — G.*

You Tell Me Your Dream by Daniels, Rice and Brown

Progressions With Mixed Chord Types

Ave Maria by Franz Schubert

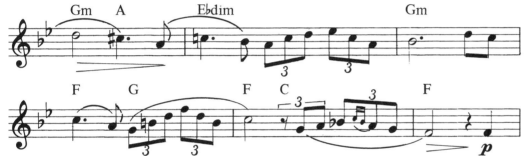

Beautiful Isle Of Somewhere by Jessie Brown Pounds and John S. Fearis

Day 22

▶ AN ALTERATION   10 MINUTES

We have one more triad to cover, and it is significantly different from all the others in that it contains neither a major nor a minor third. This chord is often indicated with the symbol sus.4 or sus., as in C sus.4 or C sus., meaning "C suspended." The chord is fully notated in this way:

The suspended chord (or suspended fourth, if you like), is aptly named. It leaves one with a "suspended" feeling, as though something else should follow. It is often "resolved" (a musical term meaning a movement that brings the harmonic tension to a peaceful resolution) by moving the voice that is on the fourth of the chord a half step down to rest on the major third:

(Another kind of suspension sometimes appears in country music. Known as a suspended 2, it places the suspension on the second of the chord rather than on the fourth. But this harmony is far less common than the suspended fourth.)

Write out the following suspended chords, then play them with their resolutions into major triads (follow the first example):

"The suspended chord is aptly named. It leaves one with the feeling something else should follow."

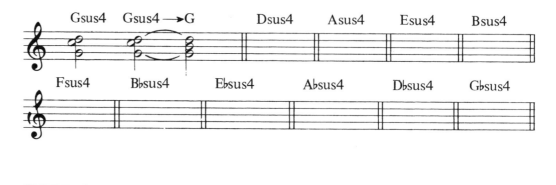

▶ ADDING MORE NOTES   10 MINUTES

So far, only three-note chords have been explored in this course (doubling any of the notes of a triad — as in playing a C on both the bottom and top of a C Major chord — does not, in musical parlance, change the chord type from a triad to a four-note chord). Now we're ready to start expanding!

The sixth of a chord is sometimes added for a softer, plusher effect. It may be added to a major triad (as in C6):

Or to a minor triad (as in Cm6):

Write out and play the following sixth chords:

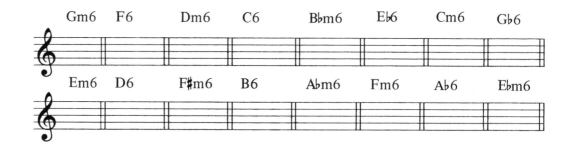

80

Day 23

▶ SIX OF ONE, A HALF DOZEN OF THE OTHER   20 MINUTES

Remember the system of counting half steps and whole steps to build chords? Let's use it once again to build both kinds of sixth chords. Starting on any pitch, we may build a major triad using the formula 2 steps + 1½ steps, then adding another whole step for the sixth:

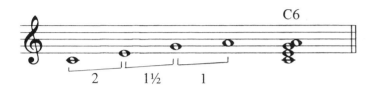

Starting on any pitch, we may build a minor triad using the formula 1½ steps + 2 steps, then adding another whole step for the sixth:

> "We can build major or minor sixth chords beginning on any pitch."

On the following six pitches, build major sixth chords using the formula outlined above:

On the following six pitches, build minor sixth chords, using the formula outlined above:

Day 24

It's time to turn to the most popular chord in popular music, the celebrity you'll find on every lead sheet and under the fingers of every cocktail lounge keyboardist from New York to Nome: the seventh chord. Actually, there are six types of seventh chords you'll find used with some frequency.

Let's look once again at a major scale to learn something about the formation of seventh chords. Adding sevenths to the triads that occur naturally on the various pitches of a major scale will result in several different chord types:

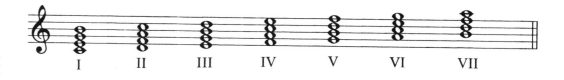

I   II   III   IV   V   VI   VII

"The most popular chord in popular music . . . You'll find it under the fingers of every cocktail keyboardist from New York to Nome."

Adding a seventh to the major triad on tone 1 of the scale produces what is known as a Major Seventh Chord — in this case, a C Major Seventh, indicated by the symbol C maj.7 or C + 7 or sometimes C $\triangle$. This type of chord is formed naturally on the I and IV in a major key (in this case, the result is C maj.7 and F maj.7).

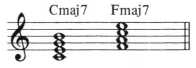

Form and play Major Seventh chords on the following roots. Just use the pitches of the major scale that begins on that root. The first two are written out for you.

To construct a Major Seventh chord on any pitch, use the formula for a major triad — 2 whole steps + 1½ steps — and add two whole steps for the seventh:

Use this formula to build Major Seventh chords on the following pitches:

Day 25

The second type of seventh chord is called the Dominant Seventh, because it is naturally formed as an extension of the V chord. (The I chord is known as the Tonic, and the V chord is known as the Dominant. So the type of Seventh Chord that occurs on the V is called a Dominant Seventh.) We've seen earlier how the V often moves to the I. The Dominant Seventh makes that movement even stronger:

> *"We've seen earlier how the V often moves to the I. The Dominant Seventh makes that movement even stronger."*

The strength of the movement is a result of the strong voice leading that takes place: the seventh of the G7 (F) moves down to the third of the C chord (E), while the third of the G7 (B) moves up to the root of the C chord (C).

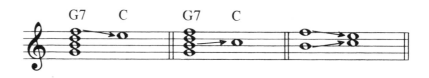

You've probably noticed that the Dominant Seventh interval is one half step shorter than the Major Seventh:

To build a Dominant Seventh chord, simply construct a major triad (2 steps + 1½ steps) and add a minor third (1½ steps) on top:

Form and play Dominant Seventh chords (indicated by the symbol 7, as in C7) on the following roots:

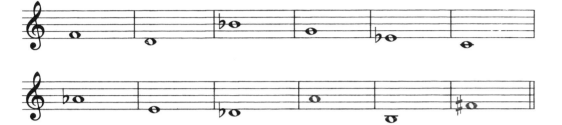

Day 26

▶ **A FANCY V-I**　　　**10 MINUTES**

Since V going to I is such a common progression, it's a good idea to use it as often as possible; it is particularly helpful in practicing the movement of seventh chords. Keeping in mind that chords may be "voiced" in different ways — with chord members distributed in various combinations across the keyboard — here are some practice routines that will demonstrate how good arrangers use seventh chords to make harmonic movement strong and smooth.

Follow the voicing in the example to play V-I progressions in the keys indicated:

"Good arrangers use seventh chords to make harmonic movement strong and smooth."

▶ **HOLD THAT TONE!**　　　**10 MINUTES**

Continue to practice V-I movements using seventh chords with the following voicing. Hold the tones that are common from one chord to the next:

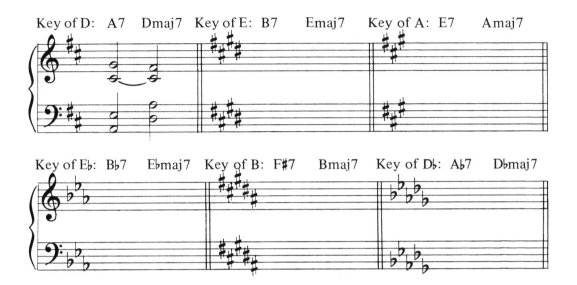

Day 27

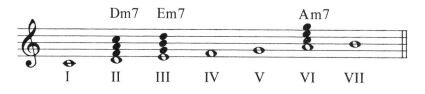

▶ THE MINOR SEVENTH   10 MINUTES

The Minor Seventh harmony occurs on chords II, III, and VI of any major key:

"This chord type occurs three times in any major key."

This chord type is simply a minor triad with a dominant seventh added (designated in pop music with the symbol m7 or min.7 or −7). It can be built by constructing a minor triad (1½ steps + 2 steps) and adding a minor third (1½ steps) on top:

Construct the following minor seventh chords by first finding the correct root for each key:

The II chord in the key of C:

The III chord in the key of F:

The VI chord in the key of G:

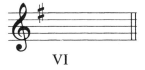

VI

The VI chord in the key of F:

VI

The III chord in the key of Bb:

III

The II chord in the key of D:

II

The VI chord in the key of Eb:

VI

The III chord in the key of D:

III

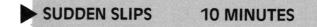

▶ **SUDDEN SLIPS**   **10 MINUTES**

Change the following seventh chords from one type to another as indicated. Play each chord before moving on to the next:

Cmaj.7 to C7:

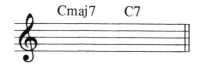

Fm7 to F7:

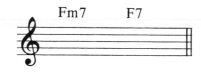

G7 to Gm7:

90

Amaj.7 to Am7:

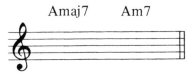

Bbm7 to Bbmaj.7:

Eb7 to Ebmaj.7:

Day 28

Here's a chord that is seldom used, but it's a good idea to review it because it does occasionally appear in popular sheet music. The minor chord with a major seventh usually occurs as the result of a moving melody line which appears over a minor harmony. It might look like this, with the movement in the soprano part:

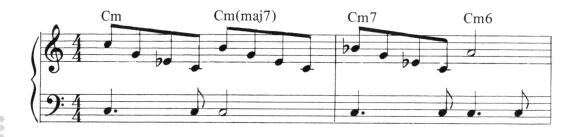

> *"Two more types of seventh chord include a seldom-used sound and a substitute for the Dominant Seventh."*

Or it might look like this example, in which the movement occurs in the bass:

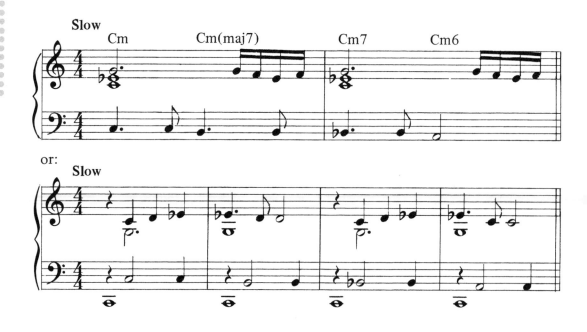

Or, a piece of music may seem to be using this harmony when it is in fact only part of the right hand voicing of another, more complicated harmony:

We'll take a brief look at such "combination" harmonies later on.
To build a minor chord with a major seventh added (indicated with the symbol m maj.7, such as Cm maj.7), construct a minor triad and add a major third (2 steps) on top:

Construct minor major seventh chords on the following pitches:

The only seventh harmony that occurs naturally within the major scale that we have not yet covered is the one that appears with the VII chord:

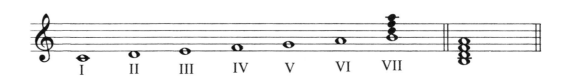

This may be seen as a diminished triad with a dominant seventh. It is in fact called a Half Diminished Seventh (often indicated by a circle with a diagonal line going through it, as in C⌀7). The reason it is not called a Diminished Seventh will become clear when we cover the Diminished Seventh chord in a short while.

The Half Diminished Seventh chord may be built by constructing a diminished chord (1½ steps + 1½ steps) and adding a dominant seventh. This time, to create a dominant seventh interval from the root it will be necessary to add 2 steps on top of the fifth of the chord, since the fifth of this chord is diminished:

This chord is often seen as a substitution for the V chord. In the key of C, for instance, the B⌀7 can often function in place of the G7 chord:

Build Half Diminished Seventh chords beginning on the following roots:

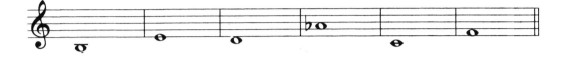

Day 29

Now that we've constructed and played five different types of seventh chords, let's put them to use in a pattern familiar to all composers and songwriters. It's called the cycle of fifths, and it will help you become adept at moving from one chord to another in the smoothest possible way!

We've seen that V goes naturally and easily to I. The cycle of fifths is based on the fact that every chord can be thought of as a I chord, and it can also be thought of as a V chord which moves toward another I. Thus, C can move to F (V-I), and then F can be thought of as the V of another chord, Bb:

"This pattern is familiar to all composers and songwriters."

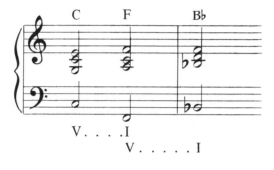

And Bb can be thought of as the V of Eb:

The cycle can take us through all twelve keys before we end up once again on C!

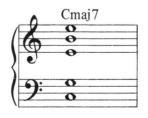

96

We can practice each of the different chord types using this cycle. For instance, here's a voicing that works well for Major Seventh Chords: 1 and 5 are in the left hand, and the right hand uses tones 3-7-3. Use it to play through the cycle of fifths by following the examples below:

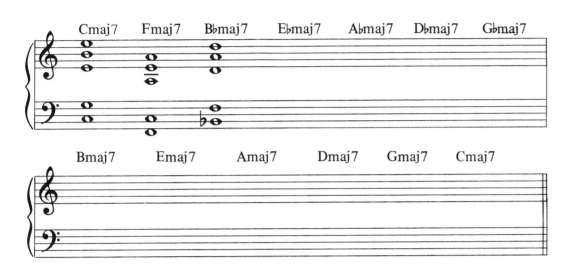

▶ SMOOTHER AND SMOOTHER   10 MINUTES

Now repeat the cycle beginning with the same voicing, but this time hold the tones common to each chord to make the movement less jarring. The cycle can be played by switching from the 3-7-3 right hand voicing to a 7-3-7 right hand voicing, as in the example below:

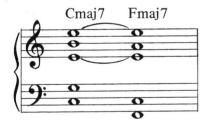

Follow these examples and complete the cycle:

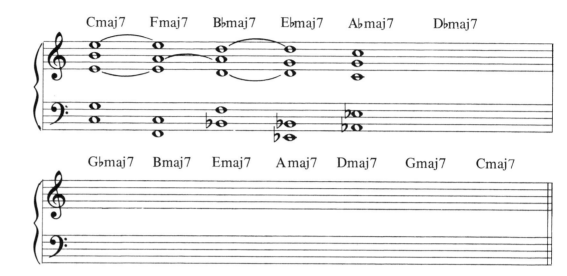

Day 30

▶ MORE CYCLES   10 MINUTES

Now play through the cycle in the same way, using the Dominant Seventh chord type:

or:

> *"Play this cycle using other harmonies, to develop greater facility in chord recognition."*

▶ A MINOR ITEM   10 MINUTES

Use the same voicing with the Minor Seventh chord type:

Day 31

▶ **GETTING CLOSER   20 MINUTES**

Before going on to our last type of seventh chord, here is a chance to use everything that has been covered, including all of the seventh harmonies, voice-leading practice and chord inversion! Our chord "voicings" up to now have been built so that there is a good deal of space between the notes. The term for this kind of voicing is "open." Now, let's make use of a "close" voicing by playing a cycle of fifths within a single key. That is, we will use only the notes found in, say, the key of C. The cycle will follow the pattern: I, IV, VII, III, VI, II, V, I.

In C, the chords will be: Cmaj7, Fmaj7, B⌀7, Em7, Am7, Dm7, G7 and, finally, Cmaj7 again.

Here is the pattern using close voicings; note the technique of holding "common" tones so that as little movement as necessary takes place from one chord to the next.

"Changing chord 'voicings' gives us a whole new look at voice-leading, inversions and more!"

After you've played through this pattern and feel comfortable with it, write it out in the following keys. Play each example after you have written it down.

101

A

G

Eb

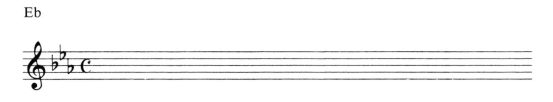

Bb

Day 32

▶ THE FINAL SEVENTH CHORD   10 MINUTES

The type of seventh chord we have not yet covered is called a Diminished Seventh, indicated by the symbol dim.7 or °7, as in Cdim.7:

To build a Diminished Seventh chord, first construct a diminished chord (a minor third + a minor third — or 1½ steps + 1½ steps) and then add another 1½ steps on top:

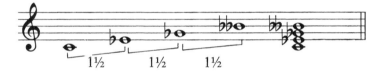

> "This final type of seventh chord has an unusual ability to move to many other harmonies."

The interval of a diminished seventh (from C to Bbb, for example) occurs as a result of taking a major seventh . . . decreasing it in size to a minor seventh . . . and then decreasing it once again:

So the term diminished refers not only to a perfect interval — such as a fifth — that has been shortened by a half step, but also to a minor interval that has been shortened by a half step.

103

Build Diminished Seventh chords beginning on the following pitches:

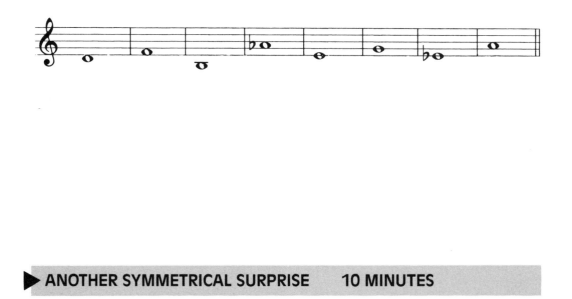

You may have noticed that the Diminished Seventh chord divides the octave into four equal parts. As a result of the symmetry this creates, there are actually only three different diminished seventh chords! The C, Eb, Gb and A Diminished Seventh chords all share the same notes (A being equivalent, on our "equally tempered" keyboards, to Bbb — a phenomenon known as "enharmonic equivalence").

This is very useful to composers and arrangers, because it gives this chord flexibility in the way it can move. A Cdim.7 chord, for example, can move to a G chord (notice how many notes it shares in common with the V7 of G, a D7 chord).

104

But it can also move to a Bb chord (notice how many notes it shares in common with the V7 of Bb, an F7 chord).

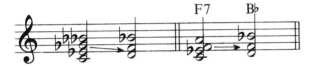

It can also move to a Db chord (notice how many notes it shares in common with the V7 of Db, an Ab chord).

And, it can move to an E chord (notice how many notes it shares in common with the V7 of E, a B7 chord).

Day 33

Adding more and more notes to our chords makes them not only richer in color, but more complicated in the relationships they may form with other chords. For example, our simple C6 chord:

"Our simple C6 may appear to be a different chord altogether when we place it in inversion."

may appear to be a different chord altogether when we place it in inversion. Put the sixth on the bottom, and it suddenly seems to be an Am7 chord!

Or, take a B⌀7 chord. Place it in first inversion and it seems to be a Dm6!

Find the "hidden" Minor Seventh chords in the following Major Sixth chords:

THAT'S A CHORD OF A DIFFERENT COLOR!   10 MINUTES

Find the "hidden" Minor Sixth chords in the following Half Diminished
Seventh chords:

Day 34

Chords with pitch numbers higher than 7 — such as 9, 11, and 13 — can be analyzed in the same way we have analyzed chords which contain tones 6 or 7. A ninth chord, for example, contains pitches 1, 3, 5, 7 and 9. There are, however, a few variations of which you should be aware.

A Major Ninth chord is a Major Seventh Chord with the ninth added:

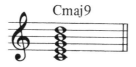

"Chords with 9, 11 and 13 are no more difficult to understand than seventh chords. Here are some examples."

A Ninth Chord — also known as a Dominant Ninth Chord — is a Dominant Seventh Chord with the ninth added:

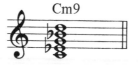

A Minor Ninth chord is a Minor Seventh Chord with the ninth added:

An Eleventh Chord usually omits the third of the chord, because pitch number 11 is simply pitch 4 (the tone used in suspended chords) placed an octave higher. Eleventh Chords use the Dominant Seventh harmony:

108

Eleventh chords, unlike suspended fourth chords, are often used to create a particular color, rather than to produce a musical tension that must be resolved. However, eleventh chords may be used as suspensions of a sort, as this theme by Tchaikovsky illustrates:

A Major Thirteenth Chord, in common usage, is either a Major Seventh chord or a Major Ninth chord with pitch number 13 (pitch 6 placed an octave higher) added:

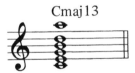

A Thirteenth Chord (without the maj. indication) is either a Dominant Seventh Chord or a Dominant Ninth Chord with the thirteenth added:

Place a correct symbol over the following chords:

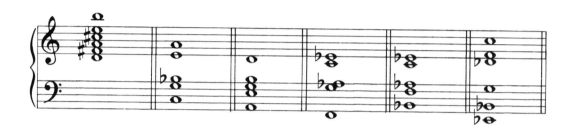

Write out the following chords in musical notation:

C13   G11   A9   Emaj13

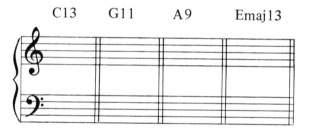

Day 35

Congratulations! At this point, all of the basic precepts of elementary keyboard harmony have been covered. We are entering the realm of advanced harmony . . .

But many contemporary pop fake books and arrangements make use of some complicated symbols that we have not covered. So this final chapter is presented as a quick overview to allow you to analyze any symbol you run into in the course of playing or studying.

Many jazz-oriented tunes, especially, will make use of what are known as "altered" chords, in which the fifth, ninth, eleventh or thirteenth will be made # or b. Here is a list of some of these chords, along with voicings to indicate the way they are usually meant to sound.

The Flat Fifth Chord is a Dominant Seventh chord in which the fifth has been flatted one half step:

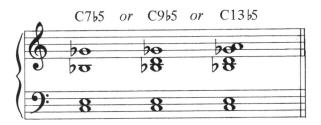

> "*Finally, here is a guide to allow you to analyze more complicated chord symbols.*"

The Flat Ninth Chord is a Dominant Seventh chord with an added ninth that is flatted one half step:

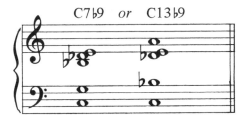

The Augmented Ninth Chord is a Dominant Seventh chord with an added ninth that is sharped one half step. It has a "funky" or "bluesy" sound because of the friction generated between the major third and the augmented ninth:

111

The Augmented Eleventh is a Dominant Ninth chord with an added eleventh that is raised one half step:

The Flat Thirteenth is a Dominant Seventh chord or a Dominant Ninth chord with an added thirteenth that is flatted one half step:

These chords should all be transposed to various roots for practice. They should also be tried in different voicings: open voicings, close voicings and inversions.

It is good to know how to decipher the musical shorthand used to describe these harmonies. In modern notation, though, these chords often appear in hidden ways. Sometimes they are indicated with a new form of shorthand known as "Slash Chord" symbols. An example might be Bb/C:

The instruction above indicates that a Bb major triad should be played over a C root. In actuality, the chord that results is simply a C11!

Similarly, if you are asked to play A7sus.4/C, the resulting chord would sound like this:

In actuality, it is a C69 — that is, a C chord with the 6 and 9 added, but without a 7. There are endless possibilities in chord symbol notation, because today many arrangers and composers want you to play specific voicings, not just particular chords. But this material really takes us beyond the goals of this volume. With the knowledge you have already gained, you can now move on to more advanced chords and harmony study without fear — you have the basics, and that's the source from which everything springs.

If you are still unclear about any section of this book, simply return to it as many times as you like. Feel free to brush up on the material periodically. Whether or not you decide to continue your study of harmony beyond this point, knowing and understanding the way chords are built and the way they move will make you a better and more productive musician. And that's something we're *all* after!

Chord Chart

Root	TRIADS			SEVENTHS				SIXTHS		NINTHS
	Major	Minor	Augmented	Dominant	Minor	Major	Diminished	Major	Minor	Dominant
C	C	Cm	C+	C7	Cm7	Cma7	Cdim7	C6	Cm6	C9
C#	C#	C#m	C#+	C#7	C#m7	C#ma7	C#dim7	C#6	C#m6	C#9
Db	Db	Dbm	Db+	Db7	Dbm7	Dbma7	Dbdim7	Db6	Dbm6	Db9
D	D	Dm	D+	D7	Dm7	Dma7	Ddim7	D6	Dm6	D9
Eb	Eb	Ebm	Eb+	Eb7	Ebm7	Ebma7	Ebdim7	Eb6	Ebm6	Eb9
E	E	Em	E+	E7	Em7	Ema7	Edim7	E6	Em6	E9
F	F	Fm	F+	F7	Fm7	Fma7	Fdim7	F6	Fm6	F9
F#	F#	F#m	F#+	F#7	F#m7	F#ma7	F#dim7	F#6	F#m6	F#9
G	G	Gm	G+	G7	Gm7	Gma7	Gdim7	G6	Gm6	G9
Ab	Ab	Abm	Ab+	Ab7	Abm7	Abma7	Abdim7	Ab6	Abm6	Ab9
A	A	Am	A+	A7	Am7	Ama7	Adim7	A6	Am6	A9
Bb	Bb	Bbm	Bb+	Bb7	Bbm7	Bbma7	Bbdim7	Bb6	Bbm6	Bb9
B	B	Bm	B+	B7	Bm7	Bma7	Bdim7	B6	Bm6	B9

Worksheet

Worksheet

Worksheet

Worksheet

Worksheet

Worksheet